# she is a daedalus



Brittney McKinley

BookLeaf Publishing

Presentation by *BookLeaf Publishing*

Web: www.bookleafpub.com

E-mail: info@bookleafpub.com

ISBN: 978-93-95950-50-3

First edition 2022

*for Katie, my built-in best friend*

*I love you :)*

# ACKNOWLEDGEMENT

Surprise! This second anthology wasn't part of the plan, but I never really stopped writing after last December. Collecting emotions and memories through mythology-inspired poetry has become an almost instant reaction now. I loved participating in the contest again, and it was so hard to keep it a secret from everyone (except Tegan, since there wasn't really a way to hide it from someone you share a studio with).

# Hestia

o Hestia, how humbly you stepped down from
olympian fame
content to tend your hearth in solitude
to make room for crashing forces of nature
but what is an ocean or a thunderstorm
a beam of moonlight or a summer's charing heat
in the face of a home's welcoming hearth

your peace and silence take my breath away
no wonders of Zeus nor tales of Hermes
compare to a home's belonging
felt in the moments between life's motion
still and quiet
slowly trickling in to fill the cracks
it glides along my heart
like the gentle pink of dawn
your powerful and gentle claim
placed on a corner of the world
subtle and warm
happening slowly and then all at once
flames flickering and dancing
as if they've spent eternity waiting to be kindled

how your hands lovingly traced
the corners of gray-speckled carpet and low
leather couches
parents kiss like college kids in the kitchen
a sister in my doorway and textbooks on my
desk
sunburned shoulders
weekends spent in murky emerald waters
a bathroom with seashells glued to the picture
frames
christmas trees dragged through the garage door
hallway walls echoing with laughter
quiet bedrooms filled with sleepy whispers

how you trailed your shadowed limbs around
a tiny, dirty apartment
with glitter in the closet and twin beds in the
next room
a kitchen with hidden bottles of vodka
music thumping upstairs
2am homework and 7am alarms
friends slide into familial roles like water
snowy boots by the kitchen door and track
spikes in a gym bag
shot glasses resting on a copy of Plato's
Republic
camaraderie binding ropes across us all
sore muscles and tired eyes meeting

mornings clutching hot mugs with heads titled together
evenings huddled on couches and beanbags

how your ember-spotted skirts swept over
the wooden floors and ikea rugs
a studio with tumbling green plants
and a  matching green duvet
a counter in the kitchen to perch on
while rice cooks and sausage snaps
a corner of the Boston skyline
glittering in both windows
instruments hung on the walls, desks shoved into corners
jewelry in a lopsided bowl from a failed pottery class
twinkling lights strung across the walls
two skylights shining on one bed
pulling us sleepily into the morning
a mug from santa fe and tea with too much honey in it
our hometown framed and hung above the TV
his books next to mine on their shelves
intimate in their jumbled genres

o Hestia, how you blessed these places
empty spaces and doorways transformed
into sacred and holy temples
hearth-flung light upon my memories

painting plaster with my shadows
great murals of moments
stretch across the walls
your dark paintbrush, my glowing pale canvas
a crooning song, an aching sonnet
I've loved my homes, so I've loved you just as
desperately

# Daedalus

an old wound
scabbed and dry
pain familiar and dulled
words spinning through the mind
impossibilities scatter and settle once more
a windy dance with well-tread steps

friendship forged from beloved steel
now a melted and misshapen structure
an ugly piece of metal
useless and upsetting and painful
a reminder of what was had and lost
at their hands and her decision
their actions and her consequence

she is a Daedalus
with her grief strapped tightly to her back
her Icarus drowning in the ocean below
tears run dry and Crete disappears
as the top of a young head
dips beneath the waves

# Hecate

Hecate follows your every step
lending and gifting her divine sorcery
I remember feeling such expansive calm
entering your realm
of unconditional adoration
her spells must have woven through your
fingertips
as you traced my features softly
in a quiet and peaceful darkness
your gentle Erebus
lulling me to sleep
enfolding me in soft sheets
tucking me in atop a gold metal frame

Hecate laid otherworldly planes
a vast empire of adventure in your home
through the trees, a sea of grass
a hill to roll down with thumping giggles
checkerboard movie rentals
little feet slapping cheap carpet
your smile knowing
another evening spent
watching princes and swans dance

a glass bowl, a bottomless rainbow of candy
vanilla ice cream on a red blanket
poolside sunscreen application
salty french fries and chlorine

if I one day have my own realm
tiny subjects running wildly
through its halls and across its floors
I pray Hecate bless my heart
with even a fraction of the magic
she imbued in you

# Psyche

o how the Romans will be wrong
centuries from now
for there is no gentle face of Cupid
no soft boyish features that will grace lofted church arches
there is only the impossible face of Eros
terrifying and consuming
a biblical fear, a devoted awe
like one of the Hebrew angels
with power sewn into his cheekbones
beauty rippling violently from his slumbering form
be not afraid, yet I quiver
candlelight flickering in my shaking palm
bathing his features from thousands of angles
each more beautiful than the last

o mystery and curiosity, captor and husband
the only thing monstrous is his beauty
no scales or talons
just downy wings lying on the sheets beside him
and an expanse of hallowed skin
he glows softly with ichor against the velvet darkness

aching pain from doubt's sickly seeds
a disease writhing into my heart
leaving fallow fields where your warmth once was
you were too good to be true
yet you're better still

this moment stretches out into infinity
sacred and forbidden
I cannot move
I could stare over your planes for lifetimes
I could lose myself in the weightlessness of you

how I am shattered apart by your sudden gaze
the fury and terror in your eyes
how I've foolishly l gutted you
forsaken trust, torn bloody soul

I'm swept away from your bedside
no longer endless but painfully finite
to meet the coldness of an olympian throne
searing seafoam eyes and a delicately curving frame

I only wish to be back in your arms
let the night forever keep you from me
as long as I may have your arms at my waist
your breath on my throat
your voice in my ear

I'll fight my way back to you if I must
with seeds and golden fleece hanging from my fingers
a crystal flask brimming in my chest
Eros, my love, forgive my mortal heart

# Sisyphus

would it be so bad to push this boulder together?
I can almost hear our laughter
echoing through stony caverns
bouncing from a looming obsidian throne
harpy screeches silenced
giving Persephone pause
regal head tilting in confusion
who laughs in the underworld?
but we never were good at being serious

would it be so bad to take turns?
shoulders braced on the rough-hewn stone
muttering nothingness between our breaths
references only we understand
a language all our own
sifting through each other's thoughts
chuckling before the joke is spoken
Tantalus complains that we exclude him

would it be so bad to sit atop our boulder?
staring out over hell
watching tartarus burn
hearing asphodel's grasses whisper
collecting gossip like puddles of water
Ixion tried to hit on who?

unbelievable, we say
roll our eyes and shake our heads
before trying to ride down again
we always fall off in giggling heaps

Sisyphus isn't a pioneer
for everyone has boulders
paths carving impossible barricades
uphill climbs and sudden plummets

but it isn't so bad
no it isn't bad at all
when I get to push mine with you
I can't imagine a better place
than by your side
sharing your burdens and lending you mine
doing the most meaningless task
tracing the most useless motions

I don't much mind where we go
only that your hand is in mine
I would cheat death twice
bring upon myself the rage of Hades
if it meant eternity wasting time with you

# Melinoë

pearly gates sound rather lonely and abstract
make me instead consort of Melinoë
a foggy specter floating and spiraling across this
plane
I would take comfort in the familiar
a creature of habit, I would haunt you all for
eternity

milky eyes landing softly upon my lineage
watching your lives unfold like fairy tales
trace lifetimes with a chilled fingertip
as they twine about one another
loving and invested voyeur that I am

I've loved stories in life, of course I crave them
in death
like absorbing fantastic tales from the pages of a
book
I would soak in the decades of stories
wonder at your plot twists
soar with Nike over your victories
weep at your side after defeat
link fingers with Aphrodite and stroll through
your love stories

I would weave the brightest fabric
speaking softly with Arachne
as glowing lifelines thread across my palms
falling into place beside one another
pulling your centuries through my loom
avid and attentive to every moment
a fond ghost, an adoring haunting

every now and then
the fates will arrive with shears
gently easing threads to a close
I would drape these completed chronicles
across my shoulders with honor
and guide you into elysian isles
your glowing golden embroidery shimmering
upon me
as we amble to your paradise

there I wish to stand, between life and death
eternal sentinel
Melinoë's torch bearer
gentle psychopomp
observing the unfolding of thousands of your
stories

# Eileithyia

I'm thinking about Rihanna and her stomach
wearing her womanhood like a luxury purse
not hiding or covering the swell of her body
not tucking away the origin of life and the point
of creation
amongst us walk goddesses
with divine universes within them

I'm thinking about dinner with a coworker's
wife
her bra size changed, but not just the cup
your ribs expand, she says
a grimace and a smile
I can't tell which one she really means
to alter and violate oneself
to become a sacred creator
am I deity or livestock
how can I feel like both at once
how can I be proud of a body
that can bless life upon empty air
and dread that same womb for its potential for
ruin me

is it vanity to want to keep my body as mine
alone

or is it my right to autonomy
is the fear of losing my youthful body
just based in pedophilic patriarchy
or is my desire to be a mother
a remnant of that same society's pressure
a singular mold
just one path ahead

I'm thinking about the man inside my head
Margaret Atwood and her eerie ponderings
how do I escape him
for even a crystal clear moment
to know with certainty what it is I actually want
instead I sit impossibly
pulling and yanking on my tired body
my mind scrambled by decades of imbibed
poison
with no way of knowing who served me the
glass

I'm thinking about my conflict not being a
choice
all these shades of gray and delicate enigmas
little glass sculptures half formed and unsure
fluttering in windows
captured sun bouncing and swaying
until they are sent crashing into violent shards
littering my windowsill under the fist of rotting
justice

black gowns with visions of red cloaks
white hoods dancing in their dreams
as they reach into my stomach
clutch my fragile and fleshy universe
and drag my writhing form into motherhood
plowing across the sharp edges of my own
indecision
my organs don their greedy fingers like fine
jewelry

I'm thinking about Eileithyia
she holds more power than any man could ever
dream
in conquering the world, they would be kings of
nothing
on thrones of barren earth with no subjects but
the dead
without her divine creation
so they place shackles on her wrists
chains around her waist
they pin her to towering white pillars
a temple to her captivity
a pyre with womb-blood dripping onto pristine
marble floors
wooden gavel splintering on impact

o Eileithyia, you parasitic miracle, you holy
virus
any shred of wonder at my potential creation
withers
as I hand you the scalpel
and beg you to remove yourself from me
before you can be taken away by force
under the cheerful waving banner of a bloody
striped flag

# Apollo

she sits on a gray couch
in the middle of the room
as her Apollo lifts a lyre from the wall
plucking slow haunting strings
notes float from his fingers
and land softly in her ears
lover-gentle and fleeting
this son of Leto and father of blessed art
ties knots of chords around her wrists
you'd think her the sailor and him the siren
her hands idle and eyes adoring
he sings her verses of honey and nectar

call this couch her stool
his music weaving through her
like the mists of Delphi
slipping into the room through cracks in reality
brought in from a much older place than this
ancient magic settling on the cushions beside her

he spins arias around their life
memories a harmony lining his voice
moments of love captured and replayed for her
a beachside bedroom
a sea of ivy and fireflies

a stone mantle in a mountain cabin
all folded into this couch beneath her
tugging and coaxing her through time

she knows soon enough this sunday afternoon
with its incense smoke and sunny beams
will be folded artfully into the tapestry he
weaves
ensconced in Phoebean melody alongside many
other serenades

she tilts a cheek and closes her eyes
content to stay forever in his musical landscape
smooth wooden guitar necks her needless cage
walls
willing captive, body held tight and languid
a statue with bliss carved into her relaxed
features

until he hangs the lyre back up
and she wakes dreamily once more
awaiting her next afternoon with Apollo

# Lethe

do you think Hades would allow me passage
if I told him about your new faces
with eyes of judgment and smiles of insincerity
do you think he would allow me to drink
from sacred Lethe's waters
to forget you?

perhaps if I told him
how you changed before my eyes
a love so special and sacred
turned gnarled and unrecognizable

if I told him
after holding your hearts through so many
fractures
how your trusted palms
familiar as a sister
ripped me apart
with casual claws
you withered me

if I lamented to him
how crippling the doubt is
with years of your advice ringing in my ears
how impossible it feels to turn away

with my happiness at stake
still I linger
as if awaiting your return
to bodies with uncanny resemblance
twisted faces and stilted conversation
I don't see you in your eyes anymore

and what if I told him about the anger
how I long to forget
how wrong it feels
to be mad, so uncontrollably mad at you
the anger sits unwieldy in my body
unnatural and unavoidable
a snake coiled in my stomach
serpent strikes defend and harm all at once
I'm unbecoming myself
and it hurts more than anything
to pick out pieces of you like rose thorns
pretty pink memories fade dull
in the face of this anger

do you think Hades would allow me passage
to take these memories away
of the years I loved you with all that I was
wash them away in Lethean tides
send them tumbling down sandy banks
would I feel peace?

I don’t think the king of the dead
would catch his eye upon me
with small mourning keens
for a friendship long dead
he turns his gaze to greater troubles
so I’ll trudge back to daylight
and wash you into my past
on my own

# Horae

so dubious they ask
how a child of evergolden warm summer
could travel east
where the clouds rage mightily
their gods must be closer to earth
such powers that besiege this soil

so furrowed their brows
why leave eternal beaches
a family and a home
for distant lands and unforgiving skies

how do I explain Auxo
no gentle sunbeams, but a thick heat
winding lazily through my city
days spent exploring lakes
soaking in her radiance
lazy basking atop warm rocks
cloying pine and lapping ripples
zac brown is on and eyes are rolled
but it's a sliver of hometown cliche
we allow ourselves
nights laying over the sheets
window down, fan turned high

we can't hold each other
so we tap toes until we fall asleep

how do I explain Carpo
Marlborough street her splotched canvas
oranges reds and browns dusting sidewalks
we take any excuse to drive up north
her breathtaking wonder
filling miles of tree branches
sweaters pulled from the back of my closet
ripped tights and hot teas in cafe windows
cool air, a crisp breath in
jars of honey and cider
apple orchard spoils collected in our cabinets

how do I explain Chione
her harsh shards, her gentle pillows
silence seeping into the cobblestones
snow lining eaves of brick history
church spires softened to dull points
string lights curling down Commonwealth
chilly walks and forgotten gloves
we hold hands inside parka pockets
yellow hockey jerseys on the television
homemade hot chocolate simmering
skiing trips with early mornings
cold nose kisses and stolen beanies

how do I explain Thallo
her rushing downpours
her rumbling ashen skies
leaving a mirrored city in her wake
twice the window panes
glittering in silver puddles
rain tapping the fire escape
leaving wet spots and smudges on glass
a blurry city skyline
our socks meeting under blankets
thunder booming distantly
shared umbrellas, boots slapping wet pavement

I cannot encapsulate the Horae
mortal words lie pale and lank
in the face of their splendor
gentle caresses and raging winds alike
I cannot bottle up my found deities
bring them before creased foreheads
how to make them understand
the beauty of sitting beside a city
as it sheds itself before your eyes

# Poseidon

Poseidon is a man made out of sandcastles and
seaweed
sandaled feet pressing into the damp beach
a golf polo wrapping his shoulders
he smells like coffee and leather
and he ambles after a toddler
throwing herself up and down the waters edge
with blonde curls tucked into a bucket hat
toes tracking miniature footprints to his side

for Poseidon is a father of young women
with the strength of hurricanes in his chest
as he rears them with love and confidence
makes nereids out of daughters and
granddaughters
teaches them to shake the earth and crumble
walls
fierce and gentle, thundering and tranquil

I used to walk with him
down the briny windswept stretch of Avila
Beach
pudgy hands returning from the surf
filled with treasures of shell and stone
I pressed handfuls of salty bounty into his palms

my trove slowly filling a plastic bucket
his smile stretching and his laugh echoing

I now tread cobbled brick streets
under soaring glass buildings
Poseidon's crashing power alive within me
with the force and inevitability of waves flowing
through my life
I think of him every time I hear an ocean wave
crash
or a swing set creak in the wind

and when I pass a seashell
on distant shores far from home
I always pick it up and take it with me
place it in a mason jar in my living room
a shrine to Poseidon and his steady presence
filling my past, present, and future
with hands full of treasures
and enough love in his heart to fill the ocean

# Limos

Limos lays scars upon our sisters
her yellowing fingernails draw their blood
leeching poison into their veins
digging into their ribs and stomachs
demanding a form of impossibility
a wispy and ever-changing silhouette

she climbs onto their chests
crooning violent whispers into their necks
unnatural disgust, misplaced hatred
she starves them until they resemble her
Ovidian verses brought to life
hollow joints and jutting hips

this creature of hunger
this maiden of vile
holding your hair back and stroking your spine
making Erysichthons of the strongest women
forcing me to watch
as she tears pieces of you away in her maw
to appease the unappeasable

I pray Demeter spare us
leash her baying hound
I beg with running eyeliner

leaning against locked bathroom doors
I plead desperately for Limos to crumble
into a dusty nothingness
so women may finally see their reflections
with eyes of kindness
with full bellies and souls

# Ligeia

Ligeia waltzes through bar dance floors
and slides out of shadowed alleys
long hair and swinging hips
fatal and alluring
a honed weapon and protector
a mother’s tragedies echoing in her ears
no longer awaiting daring ships
she stalks the night
her manicured nails dripping violence

eyes alight with the hunt
lipstick red as a sailor’s blood
a body made of curling waves
she’ll saunter past you
sisters in tow
angelic beauty drifting like sea mist
sinful intentions crashing in their eyes
she’ll press a kiss to your cheek
you look stunning tonight, darling
she slips your drink away
and hands you her own

you’ll see her disappear into dark hallways
men drifting wraith-like in her wake
her murmured songs filling their ears

lilting melody, deadly seduction
their adoration pouring onto the sticky floor
bodies frenzied, pulses racing

men are often found in the morning
drowned miles from the ocean
lips crusted with salt
forever frozen in a lust drunk smile

# Hermes

future roads don't often come to mind
youth is a cloudy and insubstantial thing
when the world is on fire
and burning brighter still

but this morning I was lying in our bed
while you were on a morning run
leaving kisses smushed
on my sleepy cheeks
for the first time there was a flash
it felt like a future, a flitting mirage
I saw what it might look like
if Hermes braided us together
made us travelers with shared paths
I saw what it might look like
to grow around one another
two trees planted too close
roots expanding and tangling in each other

hope can be a dangerous thing
in a world of apocalyptic transition
where fear can coat us
an irremovable and numbing layer
my path is muddy, my future fogged
but laying in bed this morning

on sheets that smell like you
I find that maybe I wouldn't mind
being theoretically tied up in you

# Janus

Janus stood in the park that day
both faces turned to the watery sunlight
spring in New England looked good on him
an expanse of grass tucked away
a peaceful secret slipped into the bustle
bathed in excitement and hope
fresh beginnings dripping
from budding flowers
clinging to my legs like pollen

I saw visions of a future among winding
sidewalks
reflected in his easy smile
linked arms and sighs of relief
signed papers and picnic tables
giddy faith in one another
we slid west, into a home
perched in bricks and borrowed furniture

I couldn't have seen
Janus and his face looking east
at a tree-lined railroad
cement stairs and a crosswalk
while I wasn't looking
he must've seen my tears

my knotted stomach and shaking hands
making daily pilgrimages
tracing my own dragging footsteps

green trees painted brown
I could see their bones
skeletal like me
stripped defenses, pale stillness
frost creeping along the path edges
standing sentential at my transition
god of beginnings
how pretty you gave me mine
god of endings
how ugly I walked out

# Dionysus

purple hues paint years of love
youthful adoration contained
in an oak barrel time capsule
their eyes grow grooves
around years of smiles
and echoing decades of laughter

their wedding dance floor
or the cracked white tiles of a kitchen
they don't notice a difference
and love spills unbidden over both
at the creation of a family
casks remain filled
and love goes undimmed

Aphrodite boasts of green blossoming vines
of their love in its infancy
but Dionysus aged their partnership
into a decadent wine
swirling with the sweetest notes of passion
deep violet trust
and burgundy respect

a portrait of love
silently and powerfully displaying to all

a healthy and strong connection
an immortal nectar
o how the truest of love
doesn’t fear time nor aging
as it only gets sweeter
with every year spent in oak palaces

# Dido

he stumbled upon your infant city
still building its walls
conscious of your own naivety
and man's conquering nature
you turned him away
despite his wooing advances
sweet in your throat
his tenderness a wine warming your stomach
until the sudden piercing
cupid's arrow, a passion beyond your control
no choice, agency fleeing
your story has never been your own

a woman-shaped game piece
whittled into form
positioned with strategy
made pawn by man and god alike
created and harvested for your power
Aeneas and his destiny
Virgil and his pen
your life ripped from us
for cold historical sake
Trojan curse and Roman credibility

Dido the abandoned soul
your flaming pyre rushing to meet you
Carthage disappearing in the blaze
you made your soaring escape
into a realm beyond inflicted ministrations
where you walk with Ariadne across Elysian
sand
and trade seashells with Callisto in the lapping
surf
never slave to the whims of man again

# Chione

glass trees glitter
delicate limbs tunnel above
diamond shrouds
sunlight glowing from each drop
a galaxy of daylit stars
the milky way's sister snakes above

it doesn’t feel earthly
Chione’s new planet is temporary
a quick beauty
melting away even now
no ego grasping for attention
she works quickly
in the farthest reaches
art created for no reason but her nature

we trespass
under these limbs of glass
eyes wide in wonder
tongues quiet in reverence
she wreaths crystals in the air
it seems for us alone
soft and gentle they flit
on invisible rolling waves
to land lovely on my lovers cheek

I’ll allow her affections
in return for the damp quiet paradise
she installed for us today

# Zeus

a throne of empty beer cans
Olympian expanse meets a dingy living room
your eagles tattooed on their biceps
a dangerous entitlement
an ancient and terrible power
manhood wielded with the petulance of a child
and the evil of a god

making Ios and Europas of us
reaching damned unholy hands out
grabbing blindly without privilege
king of hollow claim
god of horror
what a rotten kingdom you have built
within these walls of peeling paint
on foundations of pain and hatred
what a poisonous world you have sown
where your sons run rampant
violence clutched in their fists
like lightning bolts

# Athena

how I prayed in Athena's temples
walking quiet pathways
trailing her tree-lined halls
I worshiped nightly at her altar
another hunched disciple
tucked lovingly away
pressed between the pages of books
munk-like in quiet basements
glowing screens and rhythmic keyboards
chorus moans for Pallas and her wisdom
strike our tired thoughts with brilliance
lift our half-formed concepts into life

her robes swept between us
armored shoulders brushing spined shelves
building parthenons in young minds
molding warriors in her palms
fledgling Odysseus'
we hefted spears of iron knowledge
proud helms of silver wings donned
olive leaves littering our desktops
ideas of towering stone
cavernous plans of marble

brutal and all-consuming
this goddess and her looming temples
late evenings, early mornings
bone deep exhaustion
loss of self, nothing matters
but her books, her echoing voice
who are we without her validation
reduced to our scholarship
defined by our fleeting wisdoms
a superiority complex, an imposter syndrome
under her gaze of divine indifference
empty owl eyes staring through us

those years I spent with Athena
metamorphosing from girl to woman
guile stripped away
sharpened into honed intellect
how I learned and I lost
grew and bled at her sandaled feet
love and hatred woven at her loom
my time as adoring acolyte
trapped in armor of reverence
irrevocably shaped by her
with beautiful and terrifying hands

# Briareus

surrounding me today
strange though it sounds
are hands
pairs of hands litter this space
all familiar, all beloved
and I cannot help but think that
Briareus must've lumbered over my cradle
a massive palm gently cupping a reddened cheek
hundreds of fingers fluttering in the air as he
stood at my side
before sinking back into the earth
leaving behind the luckiest baby girl in the
world
for only fortune of mythical proportions
may explain the hands that surround me now

hands that rocked me to sleep, tucked me into
bed
hands that sifted through sandy sea shells
collected from pudgy fingers on a windy beach
hands that turned the pages, and mouthed the
words
until I could do it myself
hands that placed band aids over countless
scratches

wiped away blood and tears
hands that smoothed my bony young back
pressed love against racking sobs

hands that wrapped around my shoulders and
neck
in thumping embraces of victory
on a track, at the base of a graduation stage
sitting at a kitchen table
the words "you've been accepted"
scrolling across a laptop screen

hands that stretched thousands of miles across
the nation
to be felt even over the phone
hands that never failed to welcome me home
pressing into me in relief and happiness
after running across dozens of airport lobbies to
collapse giggling into a sister's embrace
a mother's teary hug
a father's gruff "missed ya bud"

your hands have raised me
in these small and vital acts
the person I am today was molded lovingly and
distinctly
by your titan-blessed hands
I can only hope that your sitting down at my
pottery wheel

held a quarter of the joy I experienced
learning and growing and forming
at your capable hands
if I am clay, I am far from finished
the kiln a distant and slightly terrifying thought

But I know I am facing my future
and all of its turns
with an army of many-handed warriors ready
to fight, comfort, and shove unflinchingly
through any obstacle I might face
so I would like to say thank you
for your love, your support
your laughs, your cries
but mostly, for your hands

www.ingramcontent.com/pod-product-compliance
Lightning Source LLC
Chambersburg PA
CBHW051738130826
49812CB00033B/912
*9789395950503*